Is It Living or Nonliving?

by Sheila Rivera

first step nonfiction

Lerner Publications • Minneapolis

A dog is living.

A ball is nonliving.

A plant is living.

A bike is nonliving.

A person is living.

A shoe is nonliving.

Is a tree living or nonliving?

8